PARENTING TEENAGERS

Discovering God's Way

LEMYE MANKA GWEI

PRESS

Foreword

*P*arenting has never been more challenging than what we are experiencing in our generation. Parenting teenagers is a different ball game entirely. There is a body of knowledge out there about this task that all parents of teens should access in order to be on top of the issues confronting our future generation. Manka, who is consumed with the passion to see this group grow up to maturity in the fear of the Lord and prepared for the challenges of their generation, has put together what she considered appropriate tips to help parents today.

Parenting is a full time job. This statement is meant to keep every parent awake to the responsibility of helping those in the age bracket normally referred to as "teenagers" to live a fulfilling life without the sorrows and regrets associated with negative decisions many teenagers are making today. This book is a reminder that every parent is a guide, a coach and a mentor for the children God has sent to cross our paths. To this end we need to sharpen our skills and be on the cutting edge of what it means to be parents of teens in such a challenging time like ours.

This book is recommended for parents, foster parents, teachers of teens in churches and schools, guidance counselors and everyone who interacts with teens at any level. We cannot afford to leave our future to chance.

Blessings,

Ezekiel A. Odeyemi
Special Assistant to the General Overseer (Education and Training)
The Redeemed Christian Church of God.

Acknowledgments

I thank the Almighty God for revelation and wisdom to write this book.

My sincere thanks go to Pastor Ezekiel Odeyemi for his encouragement, guidance, and prayers. Pastor (Mrs.) Esther Odeyemi, thank you for being there for me. I appreciate Pastor Jide Akiode, who encouraged me to work with the teenagers and be a part of their life, through whom I have been inspired to write this book. Many thanks to Pastor Olakorede Odutola for her encouragement and the role she played.

I am grateful to Prosper Gwei, Afayi Gwei, and Eugene Tawe, who proofread and edited the manuscript.

And to my mum, Elizabeth Gwei, and my siblings, Esther Tawe, Edith Tengen, Afayi Gwei, Kingsley Gwei, and Casey Gwei, I say a big thank you for your love, support, and prayers.

Finally, I am thankful to my children at The Redeemed Christian Church of God - House of His Glory Parish, Bonaloka, Douala, Cameroon, for their inspiration and love.

Contents

Preface

*C*hildren are a precious and special gift to us from our Most High God and Creator, just as we are to our parents and society at large. The uniqueness of this precious gift (children) compared to other desirable gifts such as electronic gadgets, cars, pets, and various possessions lies in the very fact that children don't come with an "owner's guide." Experience shows us that one can barely find parents who would say that parenting teenagers is an easy task. To a good number of parents, the experience ranges from being way too difficult to almost impossible.

Leading writers and reputable scholars have proposed many secular guidelines for parenting children, from toddlers through teenagers. While we may not settle on a particular guide to guarantee the best parenting results, the underlying truth is that the lack of an effective secular guide has exposed the limitations of man's approach to the subject. So what then is the lesson we get from this limitation and what is the way forward? What emerges from the apparent limitations of the secular approach is the unshakable position of the Word of God as the leading authority and guide to parenting. The book of Proverbs cautions us to "train up a child in the way he should go: and when he is old, he will not depart from it" (Proverbs 22:6).

Today teenagers are so vulnerable largely due to pressure exerted upon them by rapid cultural and cross-cultural dynamics and changes, exponential innovations in information technology and communication, and globalization. By following biblical prescriptions, parents will find that the teen years can be very joyful as it gives them an opportunity to see their teenagers move into adulthood with the fear of our Lord at heart. Furthermore, the teenagers will be prepared to face the challenges of our modern world. However, this crucial period can be very dangerous for parents and teenagers as parental influence and authority tends to fade, making room for that of peers, outsiders, and other environmental forces.

Parenting teenagers requires a different set of rules because during these formative years they regard themselves as adults, act like adults, and want to be treated as adults. However, they lack the experience that would otherwise provide a reference point to shield them from sudden calamity. This book is a compilation of biblically backed practices that provides guidelines on the different aspects of parenting and the parent-teenage relationship. It also covers what parents need to know about their children, how parents should relate to their children, and challenges parents face in relating with their children.

CHAPTER 1

Introduction

A teenager is defined as a person between the ages of thirteen and nineteen. However, in this book we will consider ages twelve to nineteen. A child, according to the dictionary definition, is a boy or girl, son or daughter of someone. Psalm 127:3-5 refers to children as a gift from God. It is relevant for this work to extend the above definition of a child to include all children between the ages of twelve and nineteen that are placed under one's care, supervision, or guidance irrespective of whether they are biological children or not.

Children are a gift from God and as such are very useful to their parents. It is thus relevant that children be accepted and valued for no one receives a gift and does not value it. The Bible has numerous examples of women who endured much psychological pain as a result of being barren. They cried unto the Lord and He heard them and answered them. In Genesis 21:1-7 Sarah gave birth to Isaac in her old age, and in 1 Samuel 1:9-28 Hannah cried out to the Lord for a child; God heard her cry and gave her a gift (Samuel). In Colossians 3:20 Paul tells us that children should obey their parents in everything for this pleases the Lord.

Through this book we will explore what parents need to know about their children in order to have a relationship with them that glorifies God. I pray that the Holy Spirit will speak to us as we read.

CHAPTER 2

What Parents Need To Know About Their Children

I - Love: Children want to be loved and appreciated by their parents. Everyone wants to be loved by someone. Mathew 22:37-39 commands us to love the Lord our God and to love our neighbor for love is the greatest commandment. The secret of successful relationships is love. God loved us so much that He sent His only Son to die on the cross for our sins so that if we believe in Him we will have eternal life. The Ten Commandments tell us about love. Galatians 5:22 lists love as the first fruit of the Holy Spirit. The whole chapter of 1 Corinthians 13 focuses on love. It is not by accident that the Bible puts so much emphasis on love.

Children like adults want to be loved and learn by example. As such, parents have to love each other as husband and wife in order to gain the ability to show love to their children, the love they deserve. When parents establish a culture of expressing true love for each other, it gives children a strong sense of security and a basis from which to learn. The best and safest place to demonstrate and experience this love is at home and from the parents. Once we show love to our children, they will come close to us and be able to share a lot with us. They will consider us a trusted friend who can provide godly advice and guidance. In order to establish an atmosphere of trust with our children, as parents we should:

- Love our children as they are

Children want to know they are appreciated, and this can be achieved through the love we show to them. When we appreciate our child, it brings out the best in them and shows that they are accepted. If we don't show love and appreciation especially to our daughters, it may result in them seeking love and appreciation from the wrong sources. This in turn may cause them to get hurt. As a parent, we want our children to feel loved and accepted at home. The absence of love and parental acceptance breeds feelings of rejection and erodes parent-teenager trust/relationship. The consequences could be severe including depression with lifelong effects.

- Avoid belittling our children or making fun of their mistakes

In bringing up our teenager, a parent must be aware that every human is prone to making errors, and great care must be taken in how we correct them. Correction should be done in a friendly manner and tone that suggests nothing beyond the parent's desire to redirect the child in the right direction. Parents should avoid making fun of errors and avoid embarrassing corrections in the presence of the child's friends or strangers. This tends to make a fool of our child. Positive reinforcement always begets a better outcome.

- Learn to forgive and move on

In order to build a spirit of trust and friendliness with our teenager, it is important that we learn to love and forgive. An example of a parent who loved his children is found in the parable of the prodigal son (Luke 15:11-32). Despite what the younger son did, the moment he returned home, the father— full of love for him—forgave him and received his son with love. How do we correct our children when they go wrong, and how do we expect them to react toward us?

II - Children want to know that they are listened to and understood by their parents.

It is not wrong to listen to our children or understand them. This gives us better insight into who our teenager really is. If we do not listen to our children, we will not know what is on their mind. Daughters especially will find an alternate who will listen to them, and this someone could be a boyfriend. Listening to our teenagers and letting them know we understand them fosters a bond with them, creating an atmosphere conducive to the open discussion of any topic with us.

Do not shut the child up when he/she brings up a topic for discussion or asks a question. Encourage them to talk and let them know you value their opinion by listening. Politely ask for more information and do so with wisdom. It does not imply that we are providing them with ideas of things that are incorrect. By so doing we will correct their views as well as point them in the right direction in love and understanding. The following will help us listen to our children much better:

- Give them full attention: Whenever you are talking to your children, try to give them your undivided attention. Stop anything that could be distracting like watching TV, listening to the radio, or working on the computer, any activity that could get in the way of discussing with your children. This will enhance communication and portray your commitment to understanding your child and being his/her best friend in whom he/she can confide.
- Put on a friendly look when listening to your children. Get closer to him/her and avoid unfriendly body language, such as sitting and not facing him/her, rolling your eyes, or interrupting him/her. This will create a friendly atmosphere and trust for him/her to open up.
- Listen carefully and always let your children know you understand what they are telling you and that you can feel their pain or joy. Ask questions for clarification. You may also learn something from them.

III - Children need encouragement and respect from their parents. Encourage your children by focusing on the positive while correcting the negative. If your child comes home with a B grade rather than an A, it is okay to accept, reward, and encourage them. When the teenager struggles with success, encourage them in love and make them know they are capable of succeeding. Imagine your teenager learning how to play basketball and struggling with it while other children are excelling. Encourage your child and let them know they are doing well, and maybe you can provide them with one-on-one classes with the coach to make them better. Parents can meet this need of encouragement and respect by doing the following:

- Tell them how good they are doing so far. This will make them believe in themselves and strive to do better. Look out for the strengths in your teenager and encourage them in that character. Encourage your teenager by focusing on who they are, which will also help build up their confidence and self-esteem. As they become confident in themselves and have a high self-esteem, they will be able to face life's challenges with confidence.
- Respecting your teenager does not make you inferior to them or give room for disrespect. Rather, it helps in building a relationship between the two of you.
- Be slow in anger toward your teenagers. When you experience bad behavior from your teenager, correct them calmly and in love while showing respect as well. Sometimes teenagers may fight back when they are corrected. Don't react and bring yourself down to their level. If the situation is tense, walk away to regain composure but be sure to address it, correcting them calmly, with love and respect, making your point very clear. This will win the teenager over but with the knowledge that as they grow up there are consequences for bad behavior and it will not be tolerated. Mum or Dad will not respond immediately but they will surely respond. Thus, they will always think twice before engaging in bad behavior.
- Use positive words rather than negative words on your teenagers. James 3:5-12 talks about what the tongue is capable of

doing, including setting our whole life on fire. Therefore, our tongue should be used with care. What we say can build our teenager or mar our teenager. Use words of blessing rather than curses.

- Set your expectations within your teenager's reach. Parents should understand that teenagers, as a result of their age and nature, can only do so much of certain things. It can be very discouraging to teenagers when they are always expected to measure up to standards beyond their reach. One good way of motivating and building self-esteem is to make sure that as parents we are not raising the bar too high.

IV - Spend time with your children and celebrate them.

Parents should strive to do some of those very little things in life that are so meaningful and matter so much to our teenagers. Birthdays are very important. Children want to know their parents will always remember their birthdays. If we are away from home on our teenager's birthday, we would do well to call them and if possible leave a gift for them. If we don't remember them on their birthdays, their peers, boyfriends, and girlfriends will. The result will be more closeness to their peers and friends rather than to us, their parents. They will feel more loved by others than by their parents. They will believe their peers and friends care more and accept them more than their parents. Do something special for your teenager on their birthday. Once we do that, they will always look forward to spending time at home on their birthday as they know their parents will do something special for them. This will keep them away from trouble, and we will be spending time with them, something teenagers cherish.

When we spend time with our teenager, we get to understand them and know them better. We will know their likes and dislikes; we will learn to have an open communication with them resulting in more trust between the parent and the teenager. Take them out for a walk. This is exercising as well as spending time with them. For our teenage girls, spending time with them in the kitchen will help teach them how to cook and manage the kitchen. Do different chores with them while talking and having a great time. This will help build a relationship between the parent and teenager.

To know if we are spending time with our children, it is helpful to ask ourselves some questions such as: *Within the last week, how many times have we shared a meal with our teen (family meals count too)? Within the last week, how many nights have we said "good-night" to our teen? Within the last week, how many mornings have we said "good morning" to our teen? Within the last week, how many times have we said "I love you" to our teen? How many conversations have we had with our teen in the past week (one-minute conversations count)? When is the last time we took an interest in our teen's latest book or television show?* (Questions taken from Parentingteens.about.com)

Teenagers want to know they belong to a home, and if we know what teenagers expect of us as a parent, we will be able to relate better with them by the special grace of God.

CHAPTER 3

How Parents Should Relate With Their Children

- Parents should love their children.
  Parents' love for their children should not be an option. The Bible in 1 Corinthians 13:13 tells us the greatest gift is love. If we love our children, we will exercise patience and show kindness as well as respect them, which is in accordance to the Word of God (1 Corinthians 13:4-7). Always remember that children learn from their parents. Therefore, parents should also learn to love one another and train their children to love one another by showing them love.

The Bible tells us in Titus 2:4 that older women should train younger women to love their husbands and their children. Loving our children is important for healthy relationships. This does not mean we should allow our teenagers to do as they please or disrespect us. At the same time, we should not be an authoritative parent. Not showing love to our teenager could result in them looking for love outside of the house.

There are plenty of people (bad company) out there looking to destroy the lives of teenage girls in particular. The Bible tells us in John 10:10 that the thief's purpose is to steal and kill and destroy. The devil is looking for whom to devour. Therefore, if we are not available to show love to our teenage girl, someone will replace us and the result could be bad company, running away from home, unwanted pregnancy, drugs, etc.

As parents, we need God's grace and wisdom to strike a balance and not be an authoritative parent yet on the other hand not be a permissive parent who will allow the children to get whatever they want. Parents should encourage and partner with their children rather than control them. Such a relationship will earn respect, which is critical in our relationship with our teenager. "Train up a child in the way he should go: and when he is old, he will not depart from it" (Proverbs 22:6). Training takes skill and patience and the grace of God.

When correcting your teenager, show them why the correction is necessary, what is wrong in what they did, and why it is wrong. This will help them understand the big picture of life, and they will grow up appreciating our correction and will pass it on from generation to generation.

- Parents should provide for their children.
  As a parent, we don't need to have an abundance to provide for our children. Provide the basic necessities of your children; if you don't, someone else will take your place. Daughters are especially susceptible. In 2 Corinthians 12:14, the Bible asks parents to provide for their children. Therefore, it is our godly responsibility to provide for our child. It is also our social responsibility to provide for our child. God will always provide our needs according to His riches in glory. Call upon Jehovah Jireh when in need as He is the All-Sufficient God who will provide for us. However, we also need to be obedient to His Word to reap the benefits of this provision.

- Parents should know their children's friends and if possible the parents.
  No man is an island unto himself. Our teenagers will always have friends but what kind of friends is an important aspect to know.

It is important to know the friends our teenagers hang out with in church, at school, at games, in the neighborhood, etc. Some friends are bad influences on our teenagers. Once we know who these friends are, sit down and have a discussion on those who are a bad influence to their lives. Make them understand why they are a bad influence. It is important to have a discussion rather than command them to stop relating with those friends without telling them why. However, there may be instances when, after the discussion, we have to make hard decisions prayerfully and stop our teenagers from interacting with such friends. It is better to be "safe than sorry." First Corinthians 15:33 tells us evil communication corrupts good manners.

Always allow teenagers to bring their friends to the house. Allow them to watch TV programs and movies in the home. This will enable us to know the sort of movies and programs they watch and whether they are acceptable. If not, have a discussion when correcting them so they can feel loved and engaged in making decisions. They will feel wanted and understand that we care about them.

• Parents should talk to their children about sex and marriage.
Don't shy away from discussing sex and marriage with your children. During such discussions, be open and encourage your teenager to ask whatever questions they have. It is important for our children to learn about sex and marriage from their parents rather than from peers. If they learn about sex and marriage from peers, there is the possibility that they will get incorrect information or advice.

There are situations where teenagers don't listen to their parents on such topics. Prayer is very necessary in such instances, as well as constant open discussion on the consequences of sex prior to marriage. Provide Bible passages to substantiate your discussions – 1 Corinthians 5:9, 10:8; Galatians 5:19; 1 Thessalonians 4:3). Pray that God will keep teenagers from bad company and also pray with the teenager (Psalm 14:14, 56:13).

- Parents should not compare their children with others.
  Don't compare your children with their friends or the children of your friends, neighbors, etc. God made each and every one of us with unique characteristics for a purpose. Therefore, it is not correct to compare our teenager to another teenager at home or out of the home. A teenager who is considered not to be hardworking today could be the more hardworking one tomorrow. The moment we compare one with another, the one who is considered not good enough could be damaged psychologically, leading to low self-esteem and feelings of inferiority. This could result in feelings of rejection and depression. It could also lead to hatred amongst the children and promote unhealthy relationships at home or outside the home.

  If your child comes home with a B grade, don't compare them with the friend or sibling who came home with an A grade. These children have different abilities and struggles. Encourage each of them and reward them equally.

  Also, do not correct your teenager in the presence of their friends. This makes them feel inferior and results in low self-esteem. It does not help in building a good relationship with our teenager. It widens the gap between us and our teenager. Teenagers cherish their friends, and correcting them in the presence of their friends makes them feel bitter toward us. However, don't let bad behavior go unaddressed. Correct them at home.

- Parents should keep abreast of what is going on in the "world" of their teenage children.
  It is important to know what is going on in your teenagers' lives. As a parent, we need to know the latest fashions, hairstyles, TV programs, what the teenagers like to do, and what they don't like, etc. Ask questions about their "world"; this will help in bonding with them as they will know Mum and Dad care and love them. If it is a TV program, try and watch it with them sometimes. If it is shopping, take them to the store and allow them to pick what they like.

Once we know what is happening in their world, we will be able to advise and guide them in the right path to take. If we don't understand their world it could strain our relationship with our teenager as we will be going in one direction while they are going in the opposite direction. This could result in constant friction, hatred, and loss of trust and confidence in one another.

Once we understand their world, any correction should be done through a discussion. Always engage the teenager in discussions, especially when correcting them.

CHAPTER 4

Challenges Parents Face In Relating With Their Children

- Peer pressure from friends and their influence on the lives of our children

Peer pressure seriously impacts the lives of teenagers in our world today. According to Keith Philips, author of *The Ultimate Topical Bible Guide: Bible Keys to Happier Living – Discovering Truth Series*, peer pressure is the demand to conform to the prevailing positive or negative attitudes or actions of one's peer group. Therefore, parents have the challenge to deal with the negative aspects of this pressure and its impact on the lives of their teenagers. As such, the training they give to their children as they grow up is critical. In fact, the relationship parents have with their children will play a major role in how their teenagers react to pressure from peers. If a parent does not have a good relationship with their children, peers will provide that relationship and children will start spending more time with their friends and doing the things their friends are doing.

On the other hand, a good relationship with our teenager could mitigate the pressure and influence their friends bring to bear on them. What will help them not to succumb to this pressure will be our prayers resulting in God's grace and mercy on their lives. Teach your teenagers that when confronted with pressure from their peers, their loyalty is to the Lord and His Word (Micah 7:5-7, Romans 12:2). The Bible tells us in 1 Corinthians 15:33 that evil company corrupts good character. Therefore, parents should not take it for granted. Parents should talk to their children about peer pressure using scriptures such as Proverbs 1:10, Exodus 23:2, 2 Corinthians 6:14-17, Proverbs 22:24-25, and also 2 Peter 3:17. With these scriptures, parents should let the children know why they need to be careful who they call their friends.

According to *Gale Encyclopedia of Children's Health: Peer Pressure*, "Peer pressure is the influence of a social group on an individual." Teenagers are susceptible to such pressure as they want to have the feeling of belonging. Therefore, they tend to "go with the flow" in relation to their dressing, the type of music they listen to, smoking, drugs, etc. It is typical for daughters to wear blouses that show cleavage and the belly button with a short skirt, fashions that do not reflect their upbringing. This is just to conform to the social pressure from their friends/peers. On the other hand, the boys wear trousers that are too big for them without belts so that the trousers are almost falling off. When questioned on their dressing, the teenagers will tell you it is "cool."

In a study conducted by Juliane, Anthony, and Brandon – *Author of TECH website, a website created by teenagers for teenagers and about teenagers*, peer pressure is defined as "when 'friends' persuade us to do something that we do not want to do. But maybe we want to do it, and we just don't have the courage to do it and our friends talk [us] into it." For instance, they may not like drinking alcohol and don't want to drink alcohol. But by spending much time with friends who drink alcohol, our teens are persuaded to take just a glass, and one day they will succumb to that pressure. Before you realize it they are drinking alcohol. Once teens start drinking alcohol with their friends, they are persuaded to do other things they did not want to do, such as having girlfriends/boyfriends, taking drugs, taking their parents' car without permission, etc.

Talk to your teenagers about bad company that causes them to compromise their behavior – Proverbs 12:26, 16:29, 19:27. "Train up a child in the way he should go: and when he is old, he will not depart from it" (Proverbs 22:6). Talk to your children about the sort of pressures/temptations that are out there such as drugs, parties, girlfriends/boyfriends, cigarettes, alcohol, sex, and their consequences. Be proactive in discussing these pressures with your teenagers rather than reactive. Don't wait till they have succumbed to peer pressure before you start talking to them. It is wiser to be SAFE than SORRY.

It is important for parents to have an open communication with their children to help them deal with such challenges. Open communication results in trust and the teen feels valued. Therefore, before the teen bends to social pressure they will think twice. Teach your teenagers how to stay out of such challenges – that is, by choosing their friends wisely, learning to say NO, and standing up for what they believe.

- Facing technological challenges
  Teenagers as well as adults today are faced with enormous challenges associated with advancement in information and communication technology. Teenagers have access to sophisticated communication and interactive technological devices that expose them to dangerously influential materials and concepts. Most TV channels air information (mainstream culture) that does not tie in with the teachings of the Bible. Mobile telephone devices have made it impossible for parents to screen and monitor the people connecting and talking to their teenagers. Social media has just added to the fears. Parents should be proactive in tackling this issue and make sure we educate our kids on the potential dangers modern technology exposes them to. Parents should read and monitor their teenager's Web pages, blogs, and social media like Facebook and Twitter to make sure their kids are not getting interested in watching dangerous/unproductive TV channels and programs.

Once I visited a teenager, and as I sat with her parents she went to her room and started chatting with friends on a laptop. When called to come and talk with me, she had her phone with her and continued chatting. The parents were not pleased with such behavior. However, this is the effect of technology on teenagers. Social networking has taken the place of family time and time with loved ones. As children grow up to teenagers, spend time with them at the tender ages and they will learn to spend time with you and know when to spend time with their friends. Exert some discipline on children as they grow up and they will learn to manage their time wisely, especially with respect to gadgets that are quite addictive.

Also, to avoid such challenges, get your children involved in church activities at an early age. This will enable them to spend time on the things of God rather than on technology, which can be destructive.

• Spending more time at work and other activities and less time at home with the children
In our world today, both parents are busy working very long hours while the children spend time alone in the house. In such situations, parents have little or no control over what the teenager does in their absence. Because the parents are spending less time with the children, they don't know what is going on in their lives. This results in very little communication at home, tension between parents and children, and limited love between parents and children, resulting in strained relationships.

Parents only have a wake-up call when something happens to their teenager. For instance, the mother finds out the daughter has a boyfriend and gets upset with her. The response from the daughter is, "Mum, you are never home, and this guy loves me." As a mother, how will you feel when you have such a response from your teenage daughter? Understandably, we are working so that we can take care of our children and their needs and make them comfortable. It has to be properly managed to avoid missing out in the life of our teenager.

So the challenge is how do we balance career and family? Some companies offer alternatives to working in the office. Take advantage of it if such amenities are in your place of work. If not, be sure to create time for your children. Let them know you cherish the time spent with them and would not allow anything to interfere with that time. When it is time for the kids, switch off your Blackberry and work phone to avoid interruptions. Don't take work home. If we really have to, we can work after we have spent quality time with the children, but also not to the detriment of our spouse.

Always be available for your teenager and offer them godly advice according to Proverbs 11:14 and 15:22 so they can be successful teenagers and grow in the will of God.

• Getting teenagers to open up to their parents
No one will open up to you unless you make them feel loved. Even when you make them feel loved, trust has to be earned between the two parties. It is important to have our children open up to us, but that is a major challenge in most homes today. It is also one of the major challenges parents face with their teenagers.

How we communicate with our teenager will determine if they open up to us or shut up. Do we talk at our teenager or talk to our teenager? Do we pay attention to the teenager's heart or do we pay attention to our own heart and forget about our teenager? If we want to capture the heart of our teenager, we will need to be sensitive to their heart. This will enable them to open up to us and/or have an open communication with us.

Encourage them in their endeavors and support them in what they are good at as well as what they struggle with. Celebrate with them when they do well and correct them calmly and in love. This shows respect for them. Be able to tell them you are sorry when necessary.

Allow your teenagers to stay quiet when they want to. Don't force them to talk. Respect their privacy.

- Both parents should have one voice
  Parents should learn to have one voice when talking to their children. A teenager should not go to the father and ask for something and the father allows them to have it when the mother has already said no. This is sometimes a challenge for parents. However, parents need to agree on how to respond to requests from teenage children. If our teenager finds out both parents don't have the same voice, they will manipulate their parents, which is not good. This can be avoided when parents spend more time with their children and have an open and transparent communication. With such communication, the teenager will not think of manipulating their parents.

Parents should have one voice and not give their children the opportunity to disrespect one parent or be afraid of the other parent. If Mum says no, Dad should not say yes. Both parents should discuss and agree. If parents discuss and agree after one said yes and the other said no, then the parent who said no should go back to the child and explain the change in response. This would allow the children to know that they cannot manipulate the parents because the parents will discuss all requests from the children.

The teenager is invited to a party that starts at 10 p.m., and they request permission to go to the party from their mum, who says yes. Knowing their father is a disciplinarian, they decide to wait till he is asleep so they can sneak out. Unknown to them, just at the time they are about to step out of the house, the father shows up and refuses them from going to the party. Parents should always have a stand on issues so as to avoid such conflicts.

CHAPTER 5

Key Points To Note In A
Teenage-Parent Relationship

a) Be born again

When God is in control of a situation, all is well. Therefore, to have a successful and fulfilling relationship with your teenager, the first step is to be born again. Let Jesus Christ be in control of your life and every situation. Why is this important? He has many children and is the Almighty Father. He has experience in dealing with all types of behavior from His children, both obedience and disobedience. Some of His children are respectful while others are disrespectful. Many of His children do things their way rather than put their trust in Him. It is better for parents to partner with the Most High, the Father of fathers, who will show them love and give them godly counsel on how to have a fulfilling relationship with our teenager.

The Most High will provide us with guidance, wisdom, patience, love, kindness, etc., to be able to relate well with our teenager. He is the Ancient of Days and has seen it all and knows exactly how to handle each situation. He is the omniscient and wise Parent who will give us wisdom to relate well with our teenager. As the Rose of Sharon, He will show us how to love our teenager despite their weaknesses. There will be days when you could feel overwhelmed and almost give up on your teenager. The Prince of Peace (Jehovah Shammah) is there to give you peace if you know Him and look up to Him for peace. Jehovah Rohi, the Good Shepherd, is available to guide you and show you the best path to take if you will trust in Him fully (Proverbs 3:5-6). The Lord God Almighty is always present as the omnipresent God to listen to us and guide our decisions (Psalm 32:8), even in the middle of the night when we look for our teenage child and they have sneaked out of the house to hang out with friends.

Surrender your life to Jesus Christ today if you have not already done so, and let Jehovah El-Shaddai be your Senior Partner who will guide you and direct you.

b) Invest in the life of your teenager through prayer
The Bible tells us in 1 Thessalonians 5:17 to pray without ceasing. Therefore, parents need to pray for their children without ceasing. If our children are doing well and we have a good relationship with them, it does not mean we should not pray. We need to pray so that the devil does not steal our joy and the relationship can get even better. When Jesus was leaving He prayed for His disciples (John 17) and Jesus is our role model; therefore, we must invest in the life of our teenagers by praying for them. This should not be a one-day prayer but a daily prayer. Only through prayers can we prevent the worst from happening to our teenager.

c) Speak positive words into the lives of your children
The Bible tells us there is power in the tongue – that is, words that come out of our mouth. "The tongue can bring death or life" (Proverbs 18:21a). Our child will become what we want them to be by the use of our tongue or words. Rather than curse our child with the words that proceed out of our mouth, we can bless them. In Luke 18:15-17 Jesus blessed the children. Therefore, parents should bless their children by speaking positive words into their lives.

Parents should use gentle words on their children as the Word of God tells us in Proverbs 15:4 that gentle words are a tree of life.

32

These gentle words will bring life to our teenager rather than destroy them. Correction with gentle words will show love and the teenager will have a better understanding of what was done wrong and what should have been done that is correct. Gentle words to our teenager will help build rather than destroy their self-esteem. When we think positively of ourselves we will grow to be what we think of ourselves. Therefore, it is important for parents not to speak negative words to their teenagers so as not to destroy their destiny.

Imagine going through a challenging time and reading Jeremiah 29:11, which says that God has a plan for us to prosper us and not to frustrate us, and to bring us to an expected end. This will encourage us and we will feel much better. Our teenagers also need such encouragement rather than rebuke. If the prodigal son had returned and all he got from his father was rebuke, he probably would have ended up a wayward child and perished. But the love shown to him by his father with kind words greatly changed his life for the better. Using negative words on your child will take the teenager further away from you. Speak positive words to them in love and they will draw closer to you; you will both enjoy the relationship God has blessed you with as parents and children.

Parents, I pray that God will give us the grace to speak positive words into the lives of our teenagers and we will not regret it as we return all glory to our God and Father.

d) Don't give up on your teenager
Despite the actions of our children, please don't be discouraged and allow negativity from others to affect the love you have for your children. Many times we look at our wayward children and compare them with the children of others. This results in our being depressed and giving up on our children. As a child of God, we will know to pray more for that child rather than give up. Did Jesus give up on us? Why give up on our child? Accept the teenager and remember that nothing is impossible with God. God can change every wayward child into a STAR for the glory

of His name. This child we want to give up on could become the one who will assist us in our old age.

Sometimes when we are pressed from every direction because of the actions of our teenagers, we go to our friends and peers for advice. We should be careful where we go for advice. Who can give us better counsel than God our Creator who knows it all and knows all about us? Retreat and spend time with God. Pour your heart out to God and ask Him for guidance and counsel. He will not fail you and He will not abandon you to deal with your situation alone. He is omnipresent and omniscient. His telephone line is never busy. Call upon Him and He will answer you. Yes, you may want to talk to someone. Prayerfully ask God to direct you to the appropriate person who can give you godly counsel.

e) Always stay connected to God
God is our source of strength, peace, wisdom, patience, etc. Therefore, to have a successful relationship with our teenage children, we need to stay connected to the God who is our Teacher and the Father of all fathers. He is the King of kings and Lord of lords. He will see us through our relationship with our teenager and we will never regret. If electrical equipment is not connected to the source of power, it cannot function. As such, to have a successful relationship with our teenager, we must stay connected to God who is the source of all we need to be successful. Do not neglect your teenager who is not walking faithfully with the Lord. Team up with him or her and bring the wayward teenager into that godly family circle as the grace of God leads. May God help you in Jesus' name.

f) Finally, parents should also pray for themselves in order to be good examples
The teenage life can be very complicated compared to when parents were growing up. Therefore, we need divine wisdom in parenting our children. James 1:5 says that "if any of you lack wisdom, let him ask of God, that giveth to all men liberally, and upbraideth not; and it shall be given him." What this means is

that we can ask God for wisdom on parenting our children and He will give it to us. If we stay connected to Him, He will stay connected to us, and whatever we ask in His name, He will provide according to John 15:7. Prayer is the master key which opens all doors. As we invest in the lives of our children through prayer we also need to invest in our lives by praying. We cannot do it by our might, but according to Philippians 4:13 we can succeed in parenting with the help of Christ Jesus, who will give us the strength we need.

GOD BLESS YOU

Epilogue

PRAYER POINTS

As a parent, if you feel God has spoken to you through this book and you want a change in your life and the lives of your children, pray the below prayer points in faith.

1) Thank You, Lord, for giving me the gift of children.
2) I thank You for speaking to me through this book.
3) Father, have mercy on me where I have failed in my responsibility as a parent.
4) Father, grant me wisdom and humility as I carry out my duties as a parent.
5) Father, give me the grace not to relent in prayer for myself and for my children.
6) Father, grant me the grace I need to understand my children and to recognize that they are all unique.
7) Father, grant me the grace to love my children as they are.
8) Father, grant me the grace to correct/discipline my children in love and in the fear of the Lord.
9) Father, I ask that You separate my children from every unfriendly friend.
10) Father, I pray that You will grant my children the wisdom they need to go through life.
11) Father, grant me the grace to bring up my children in the fear of the Lord.

12) Father, I ask that You will protect my children and keep evil far away from them.
13) Thank You, Father, for Your love and mercies.
14) Thank You, Lord, for answered prayers.

Notes

Chapter 2: What Parents Need to Know about Their Children
- Questions on spending time with your teen are taken from the URL:

Parentingteens.about.com/library/sp/quiz/spendingtime/bltimeteens.htm

Chapter 4: Challenges Parents Face in Relating with Their Children
- *The Ultimate Topical Bible Guide: Bible keys to happier living* by Keith Phillips
- *Gale Encyclopedia of Children's Health: Peer Pressure* – online article by Ken R. Wells
- *Peer Pressure – The Good & the Bad* by Julian, Anthony, Brandon (revised August 16, 1996)
- [1]*Have a New Teenager by Friday by Dr. Kevin Leman. p.63*

CPSIA information can be obtained at www.ICGtesting.com
Printed in the USA
BVOW011923150812

297985BV00001B/75/P